O! None, unless this miracle might,
That in BLACK INK MY LOVE MAY STILL SHINE BRIGHT.
— WILLIAM SHAKESPEARE

The Joining

The Unholy King

The Creep

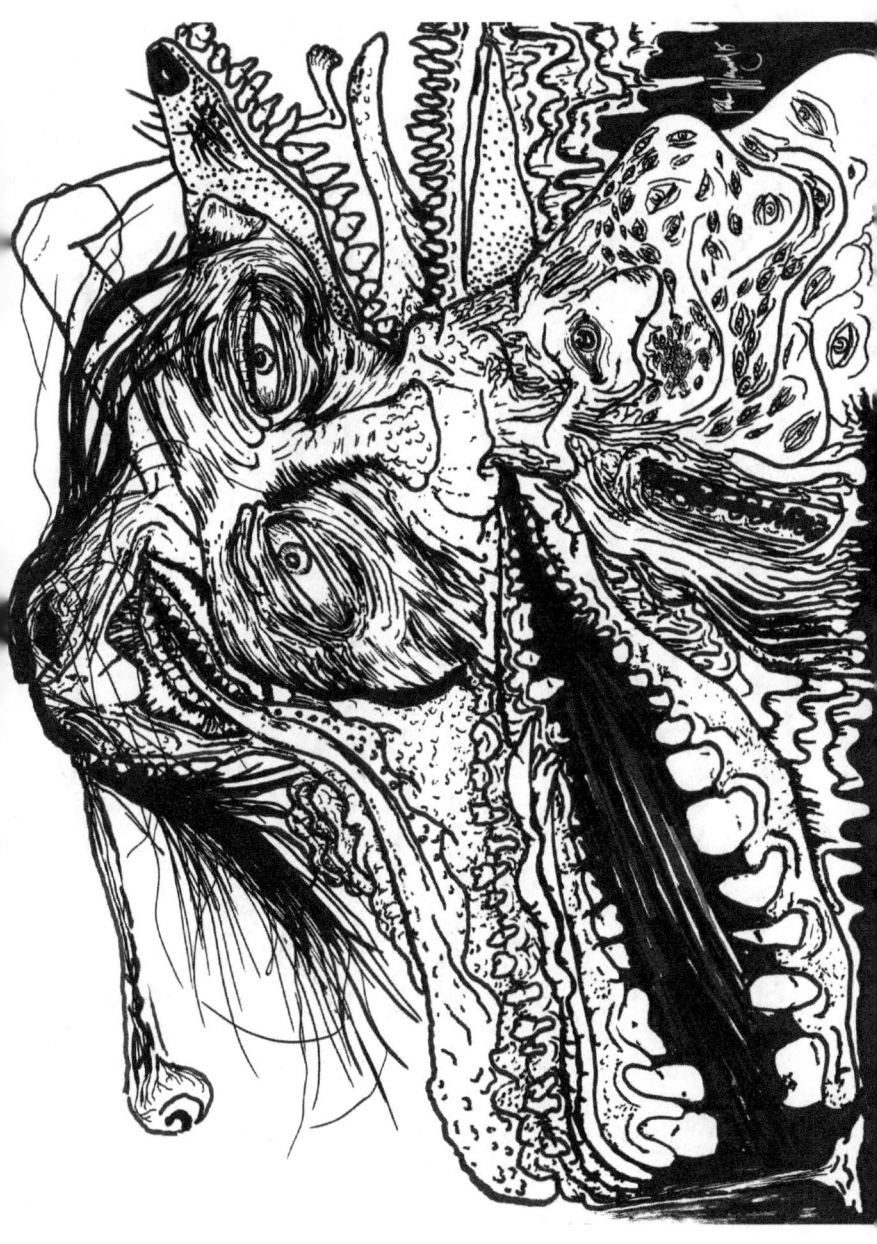

The Word

The Bath

The Guillotine

The Family

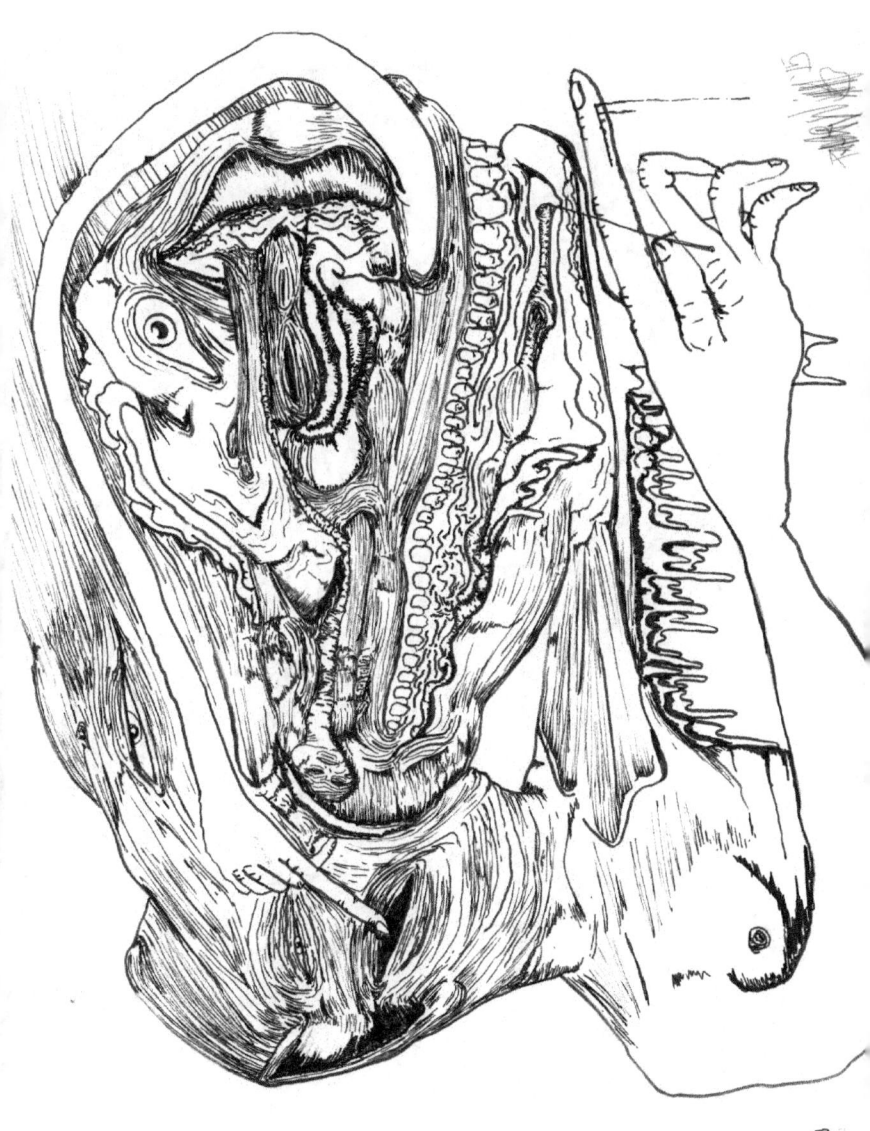

The Itch (Pointing Fingers)

The Knives

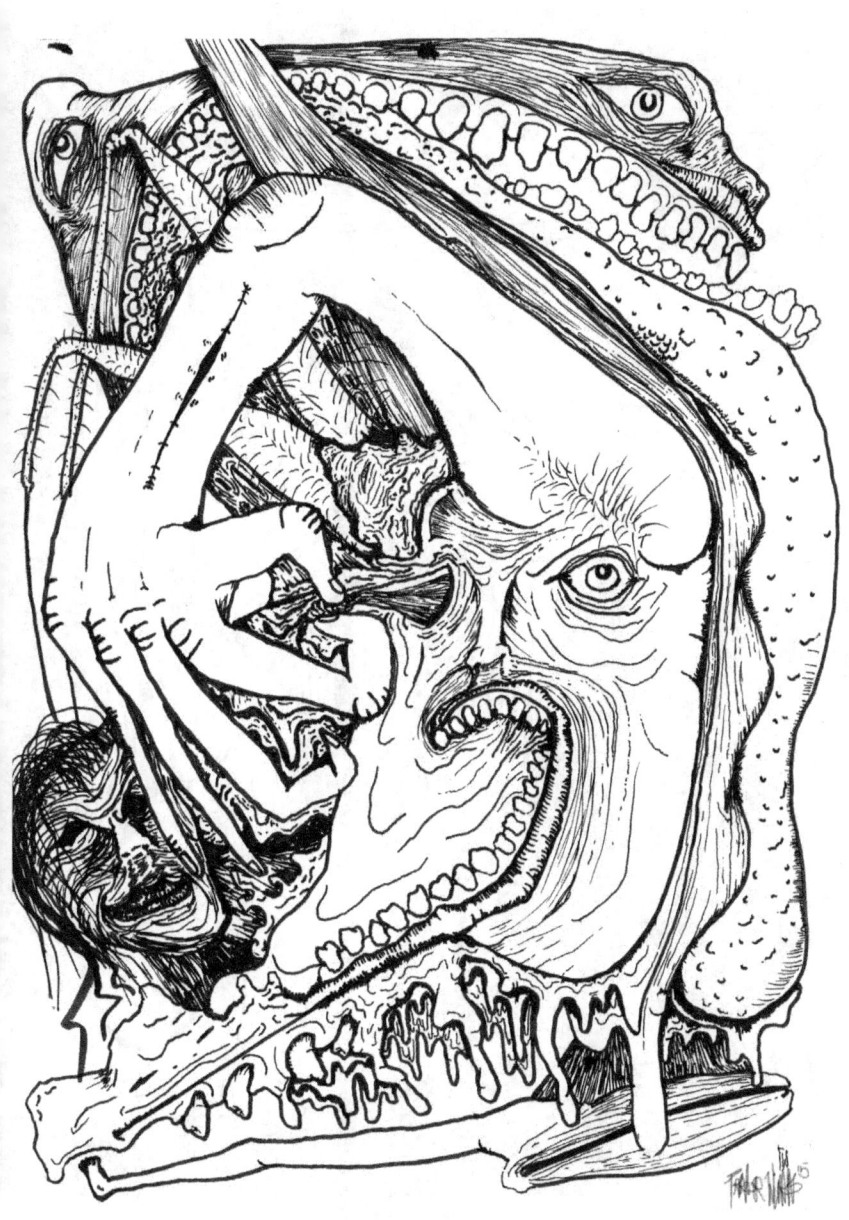

The Trick

The Rash

The Tune

The Gardener

The Call

Lost In Thought

Mr. Scumchoir

Tears

I Rest

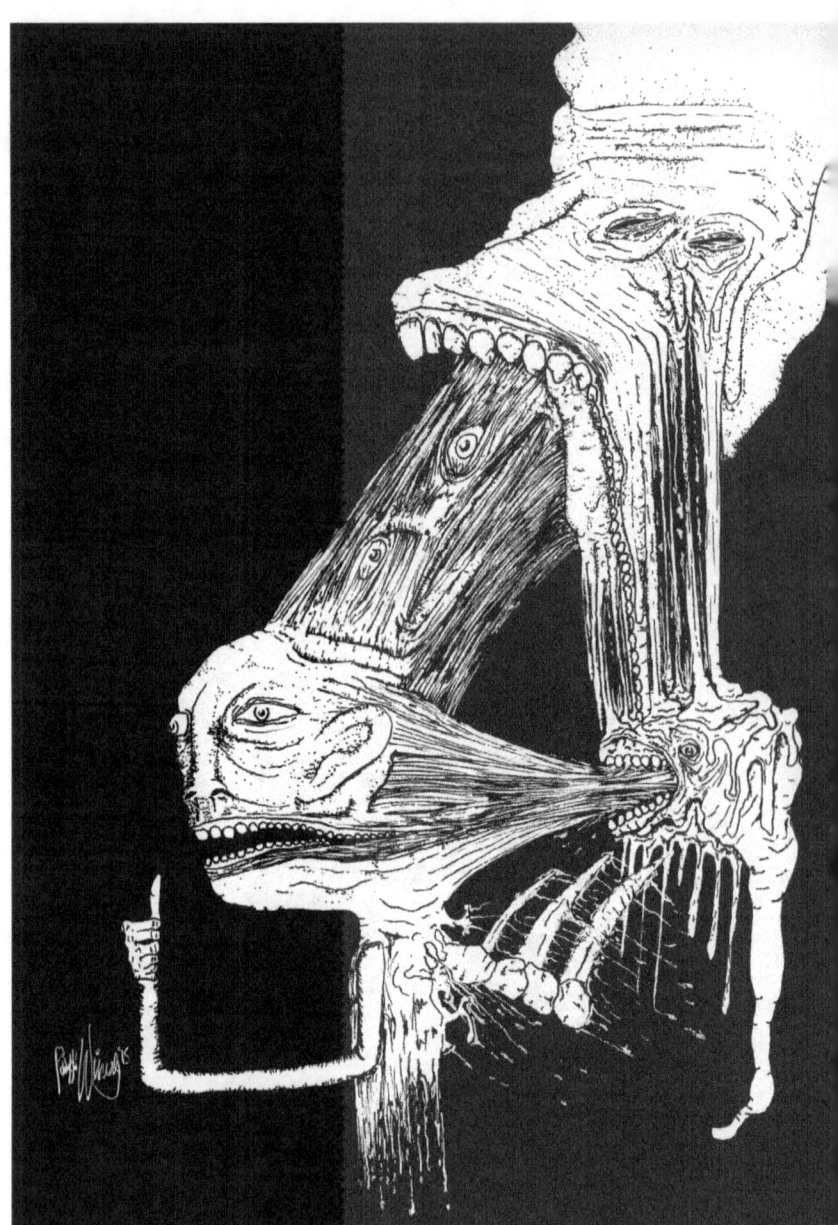

Okay

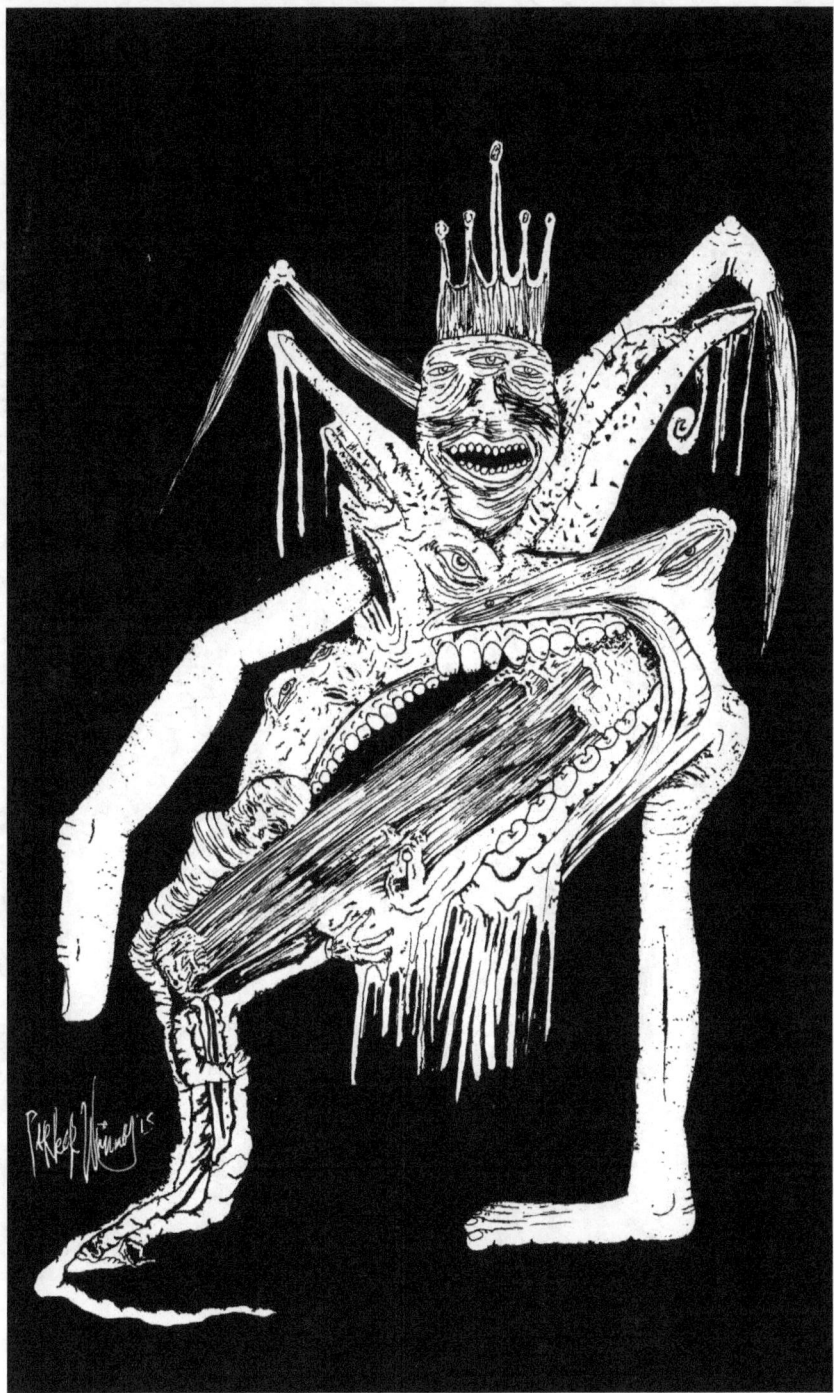

Reaching for the Key

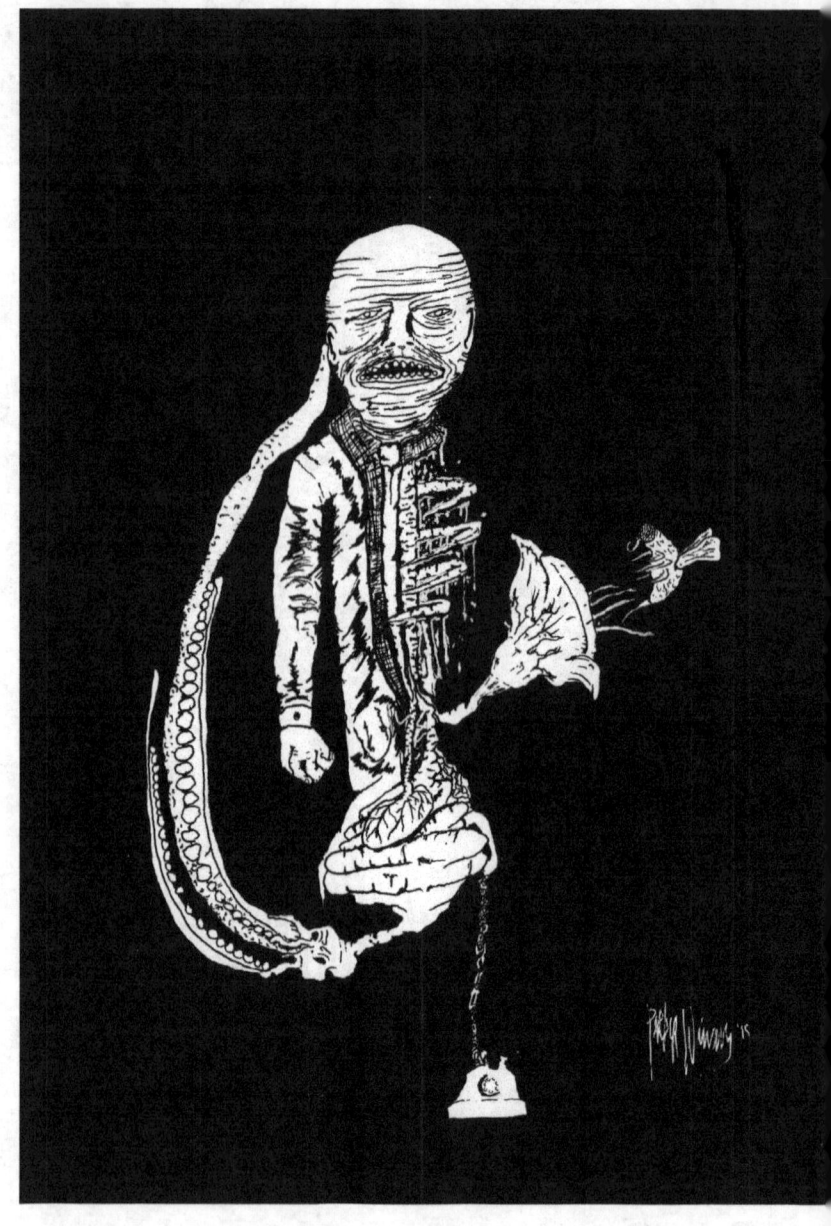

The Hang Up

The Friend

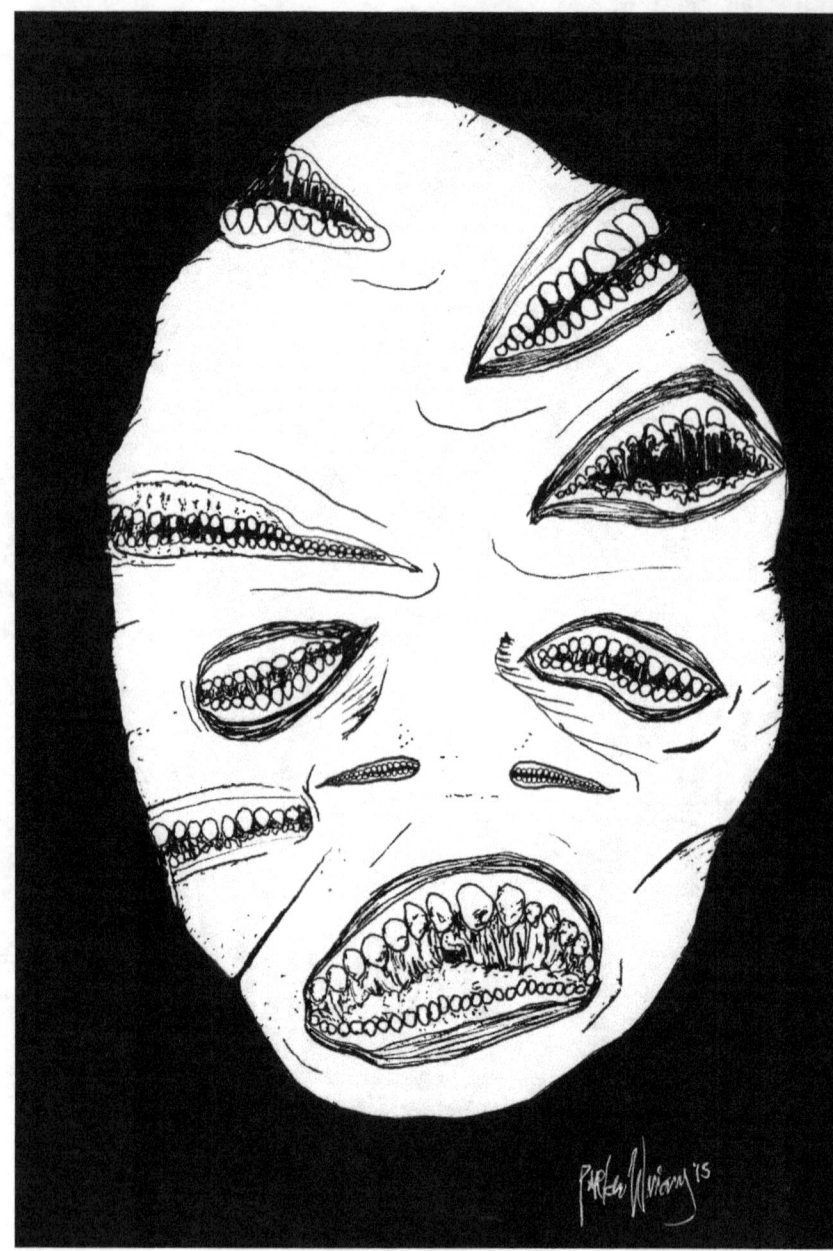

The Feeding

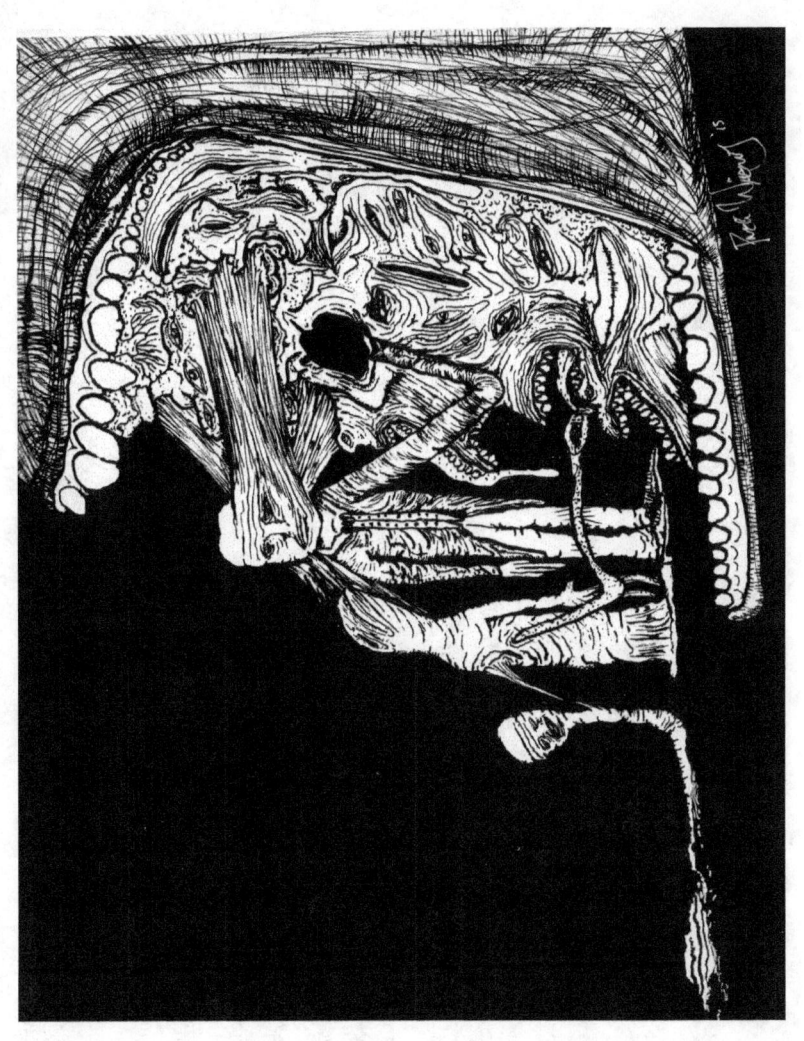

Evolving

Wednesday

The Tongue

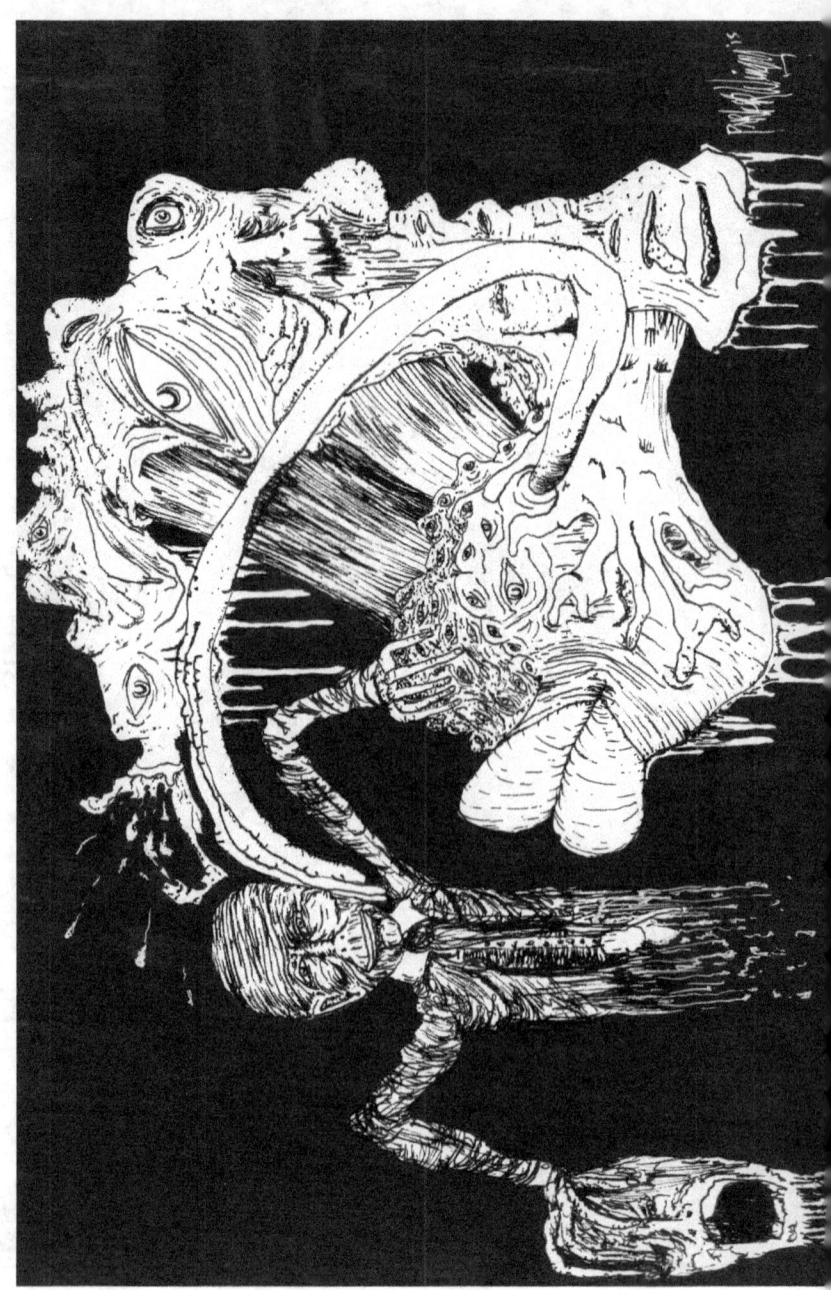

Severed

The Night Bath

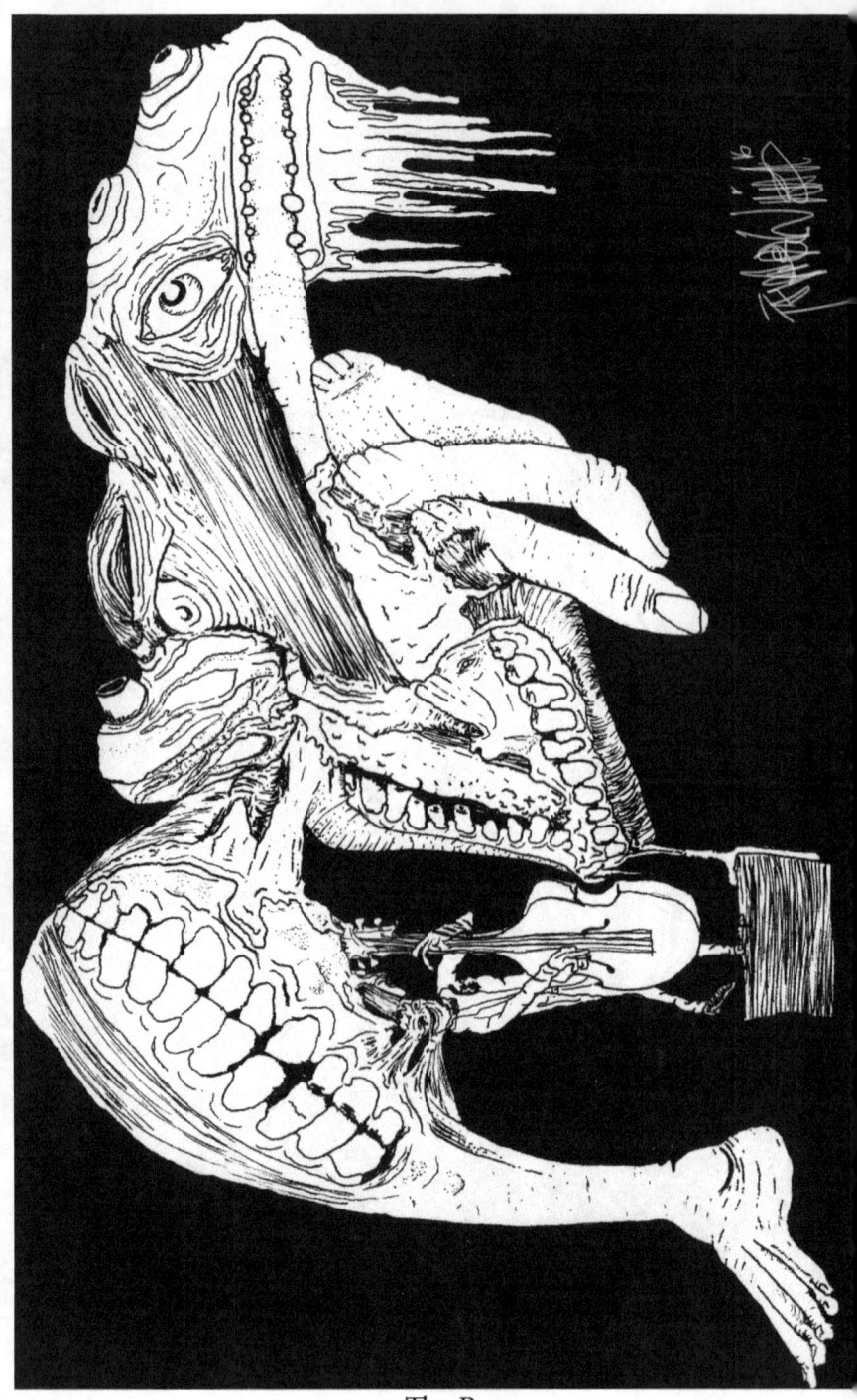

The Bass

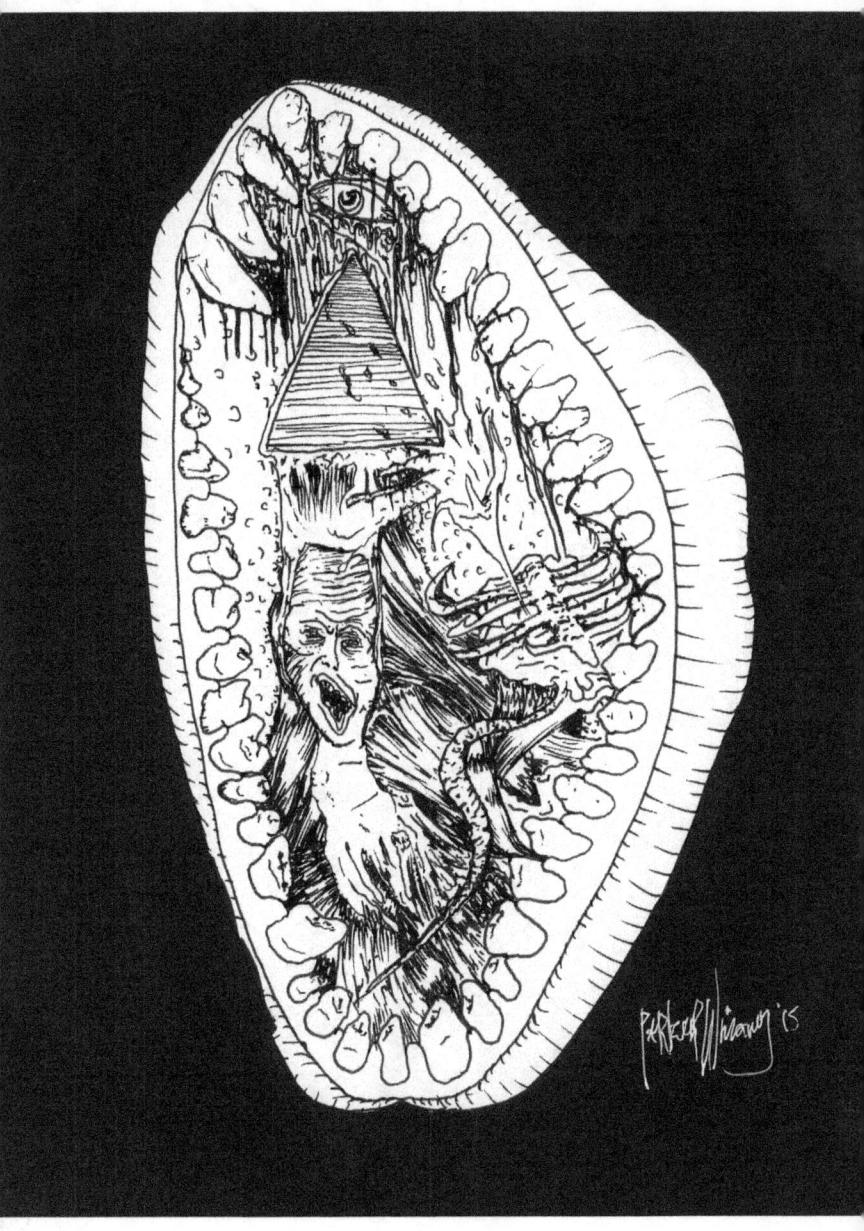

The Illuminati

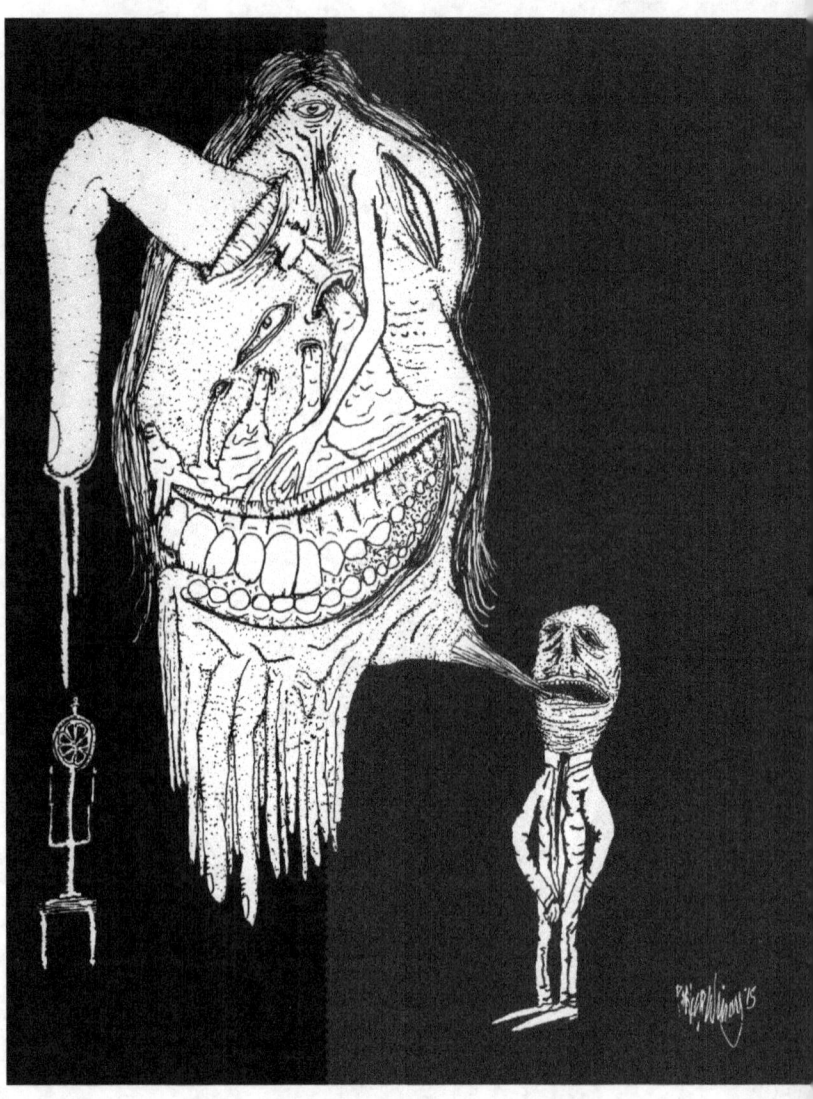

The Alter

Hold Me

Mountain Dweller

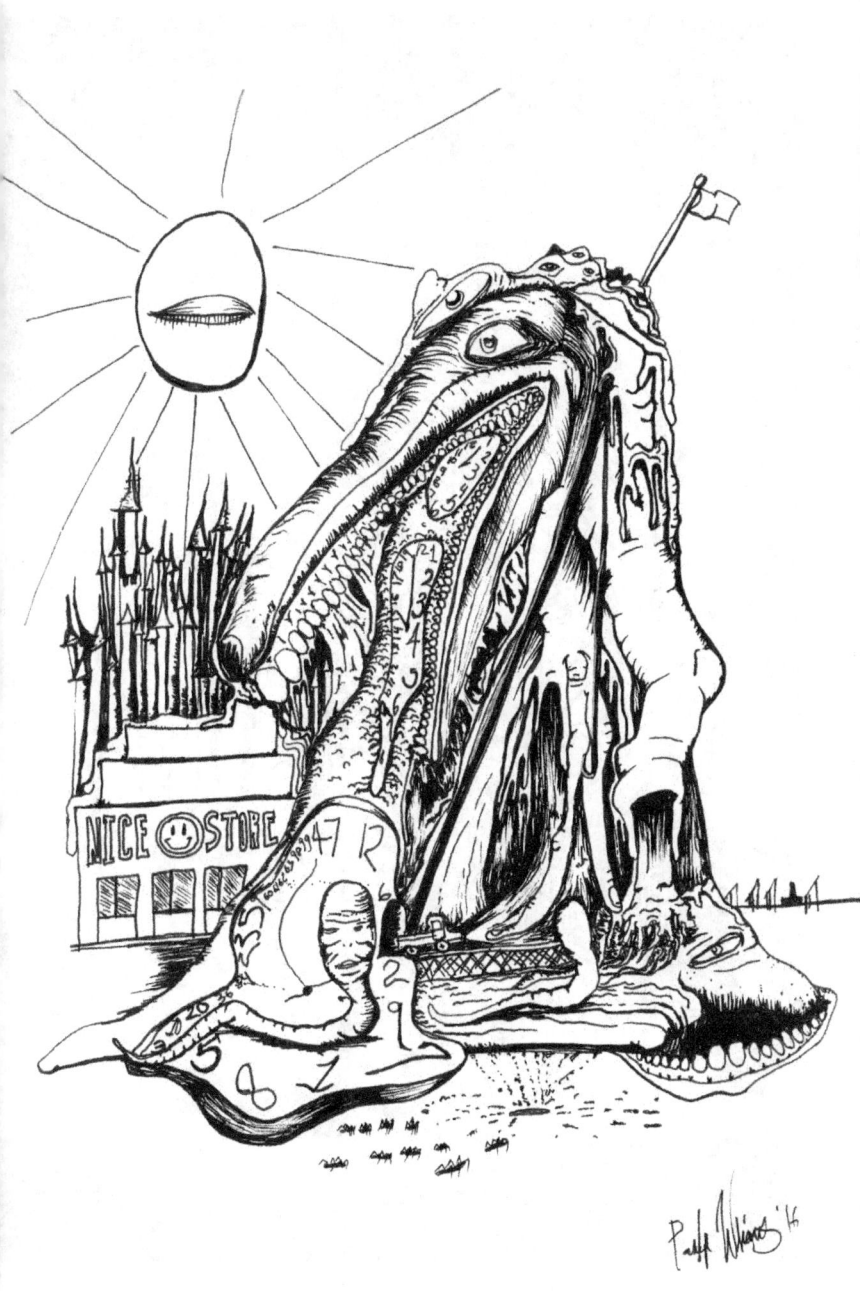

My Corporate Job

Lunchtime at the Hive

Old Man

Little Brother

I'm Hungry

Reflection 1 of the 2016 presidential election

Reflection 2 of the 2016 Election: No way to vote against them

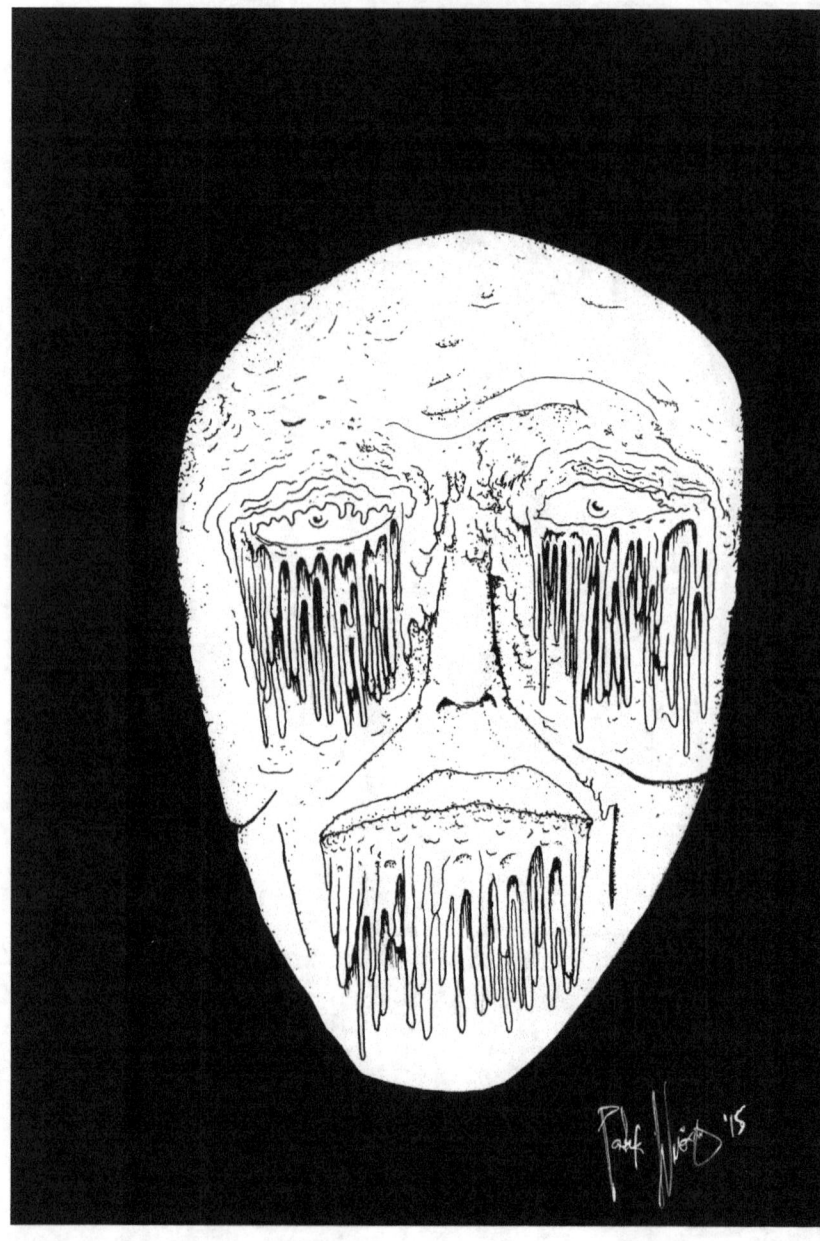

Melt

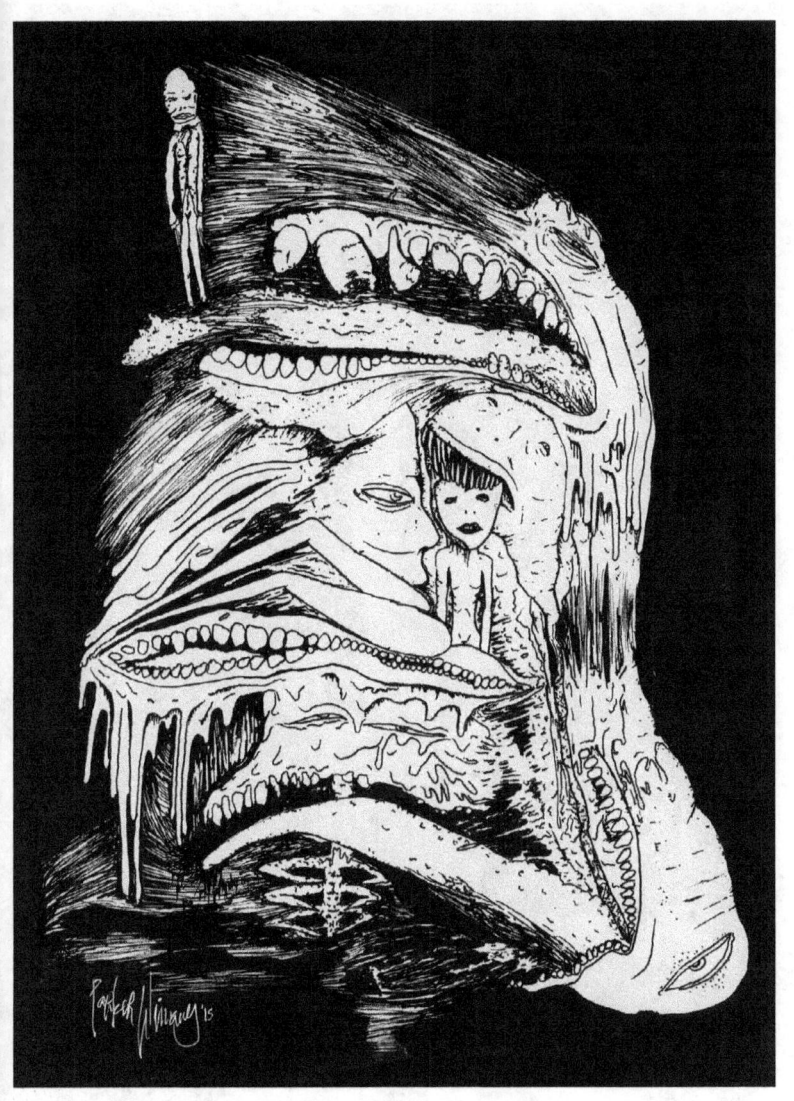

The Dream Watches

The Right Food

Reflection 3 of the 2016 Presidential Election - DNC "You Can't Always Get What you Want"

The Earth, The People, The Sun

Plant Based Diet

Attitude

Man Eating His Son

Eve

Eden

Satanic Nympho

Reflection 4 of the 2016 Presidential Election: The Most Destructive form of Entertainment

Reflection 5 of 2016 Presidential Election RNC: I'll Destroy more than anyone else on this Stage

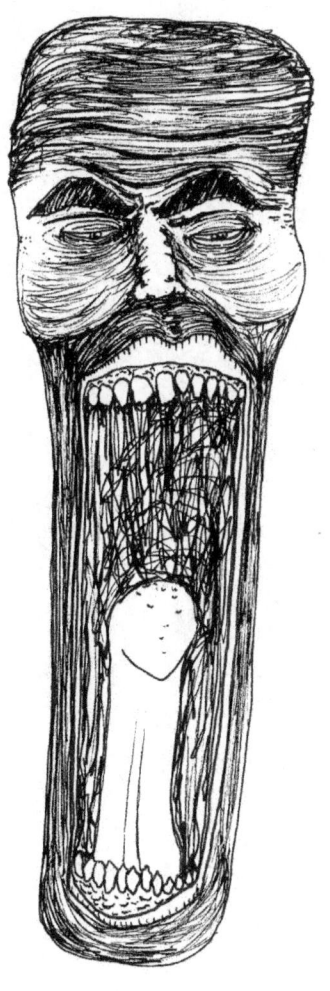

ahhhhhhhh!

Mozart Exultation

One with All

I Eat Chicken

Out of Body

Beach Girl

Laughter

My Monkey Brain

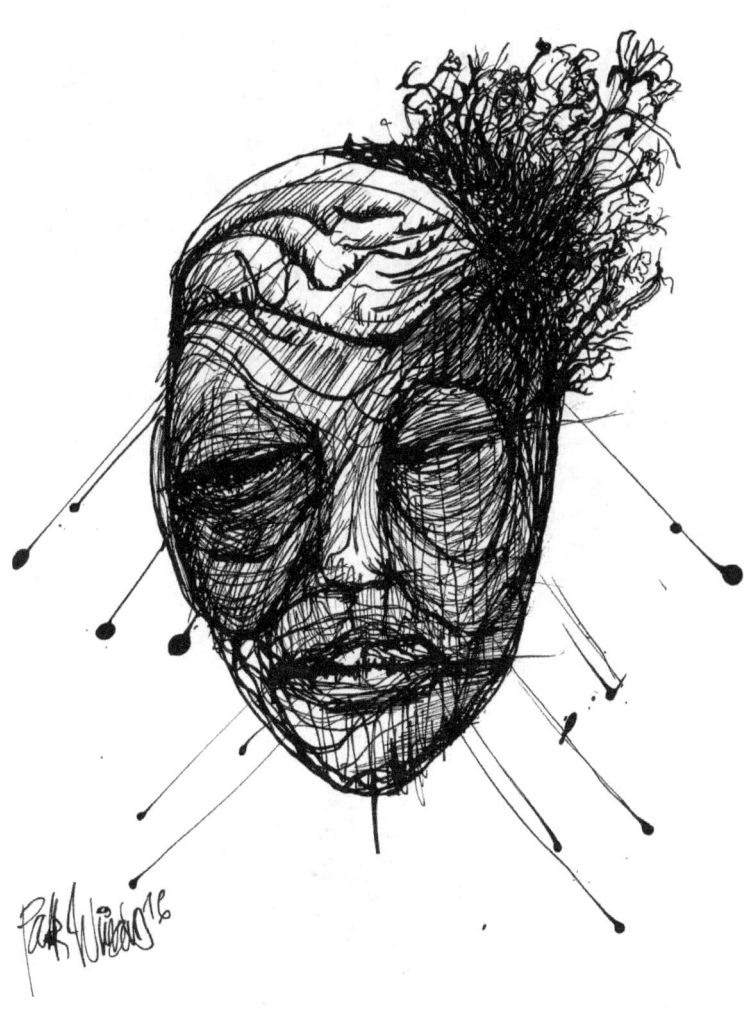

My Vegetable Brain

New King

Party People

Disaster

Nationalism: It's all about you

Temptation

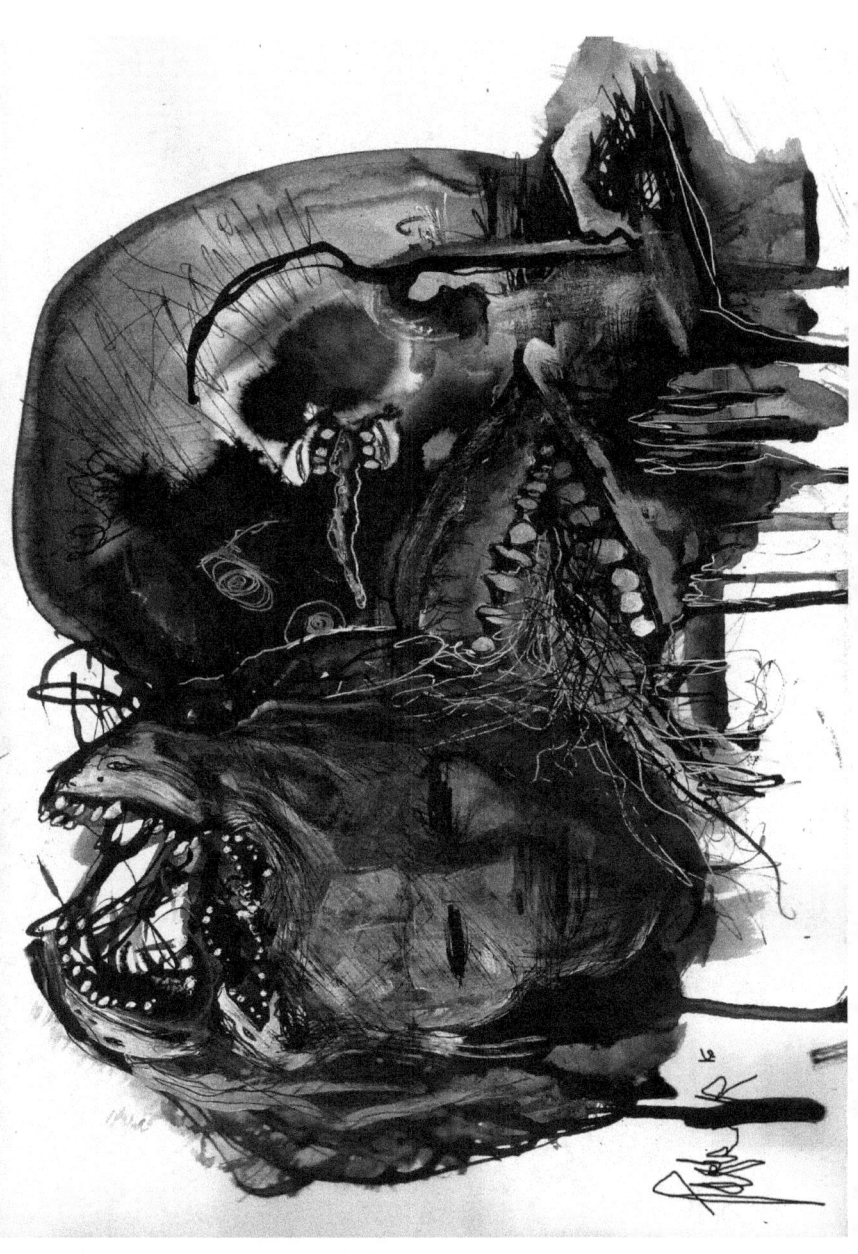

Professional Celebrity: Illustration from Easter Bunnies and Swastikas (EBS)

Bed: Illustration from EBS

TV is Garbage: Illustration from EBS

Pancakes and Booze Art Show

Debate: Reflection 6 from 2016 Election

Propaganda

Main Street U.S.A.

The Grandma

Man Playing Guitar

Morning Portrait

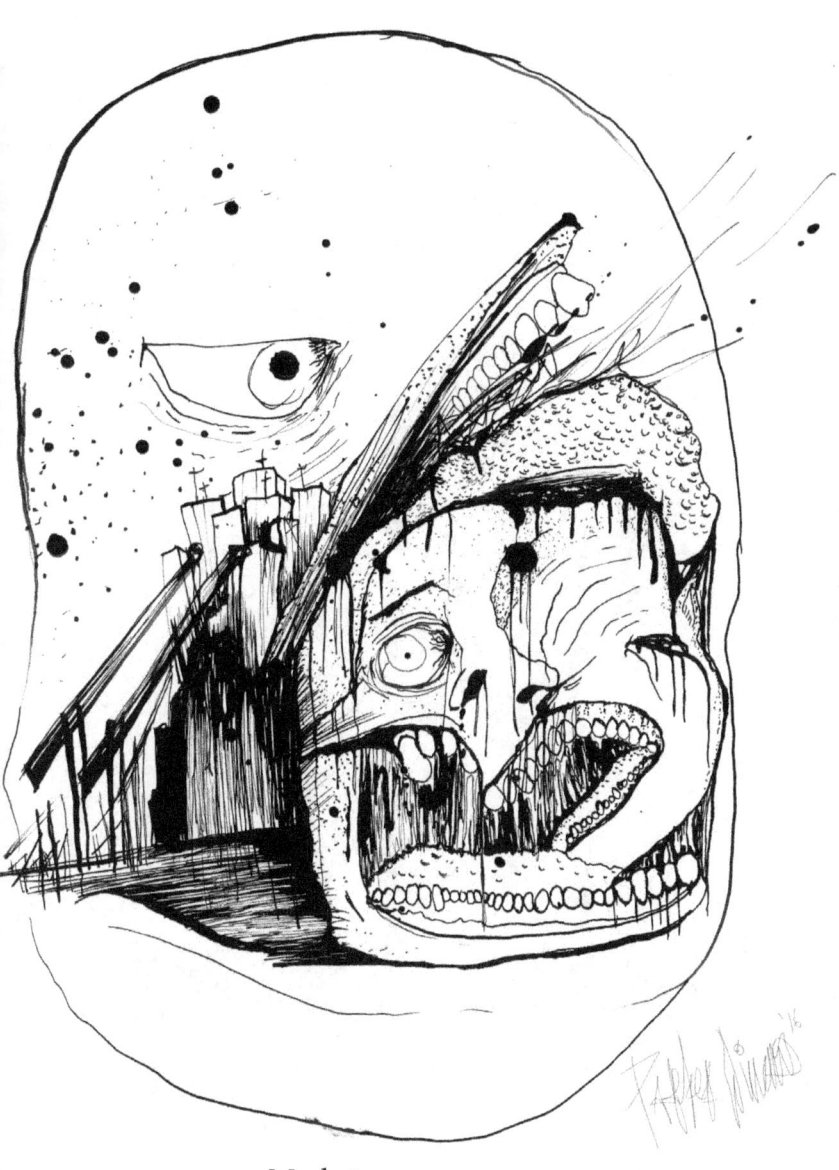

Markets

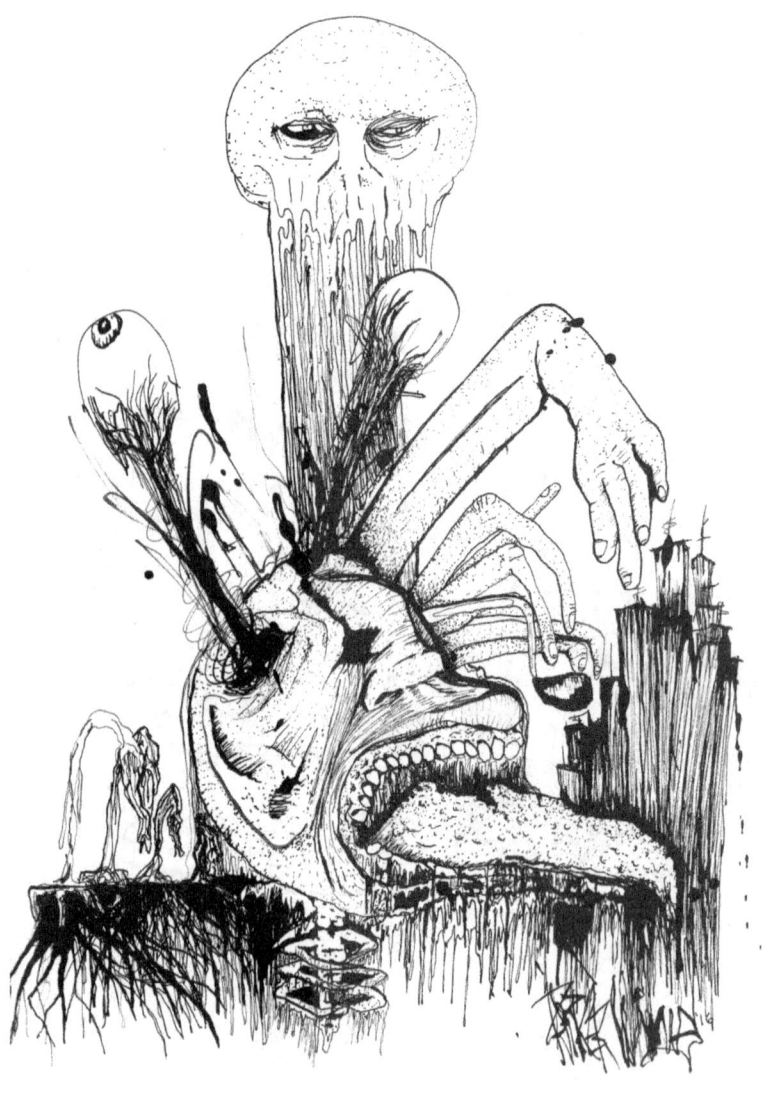

Under the Sun

the Crank

Smoke Break

The Artist

Ego Maniac

Kingdom

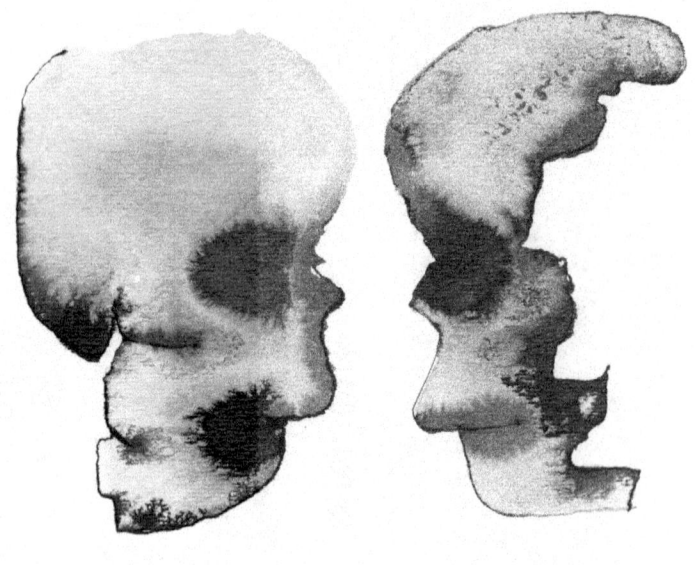

New Lovers

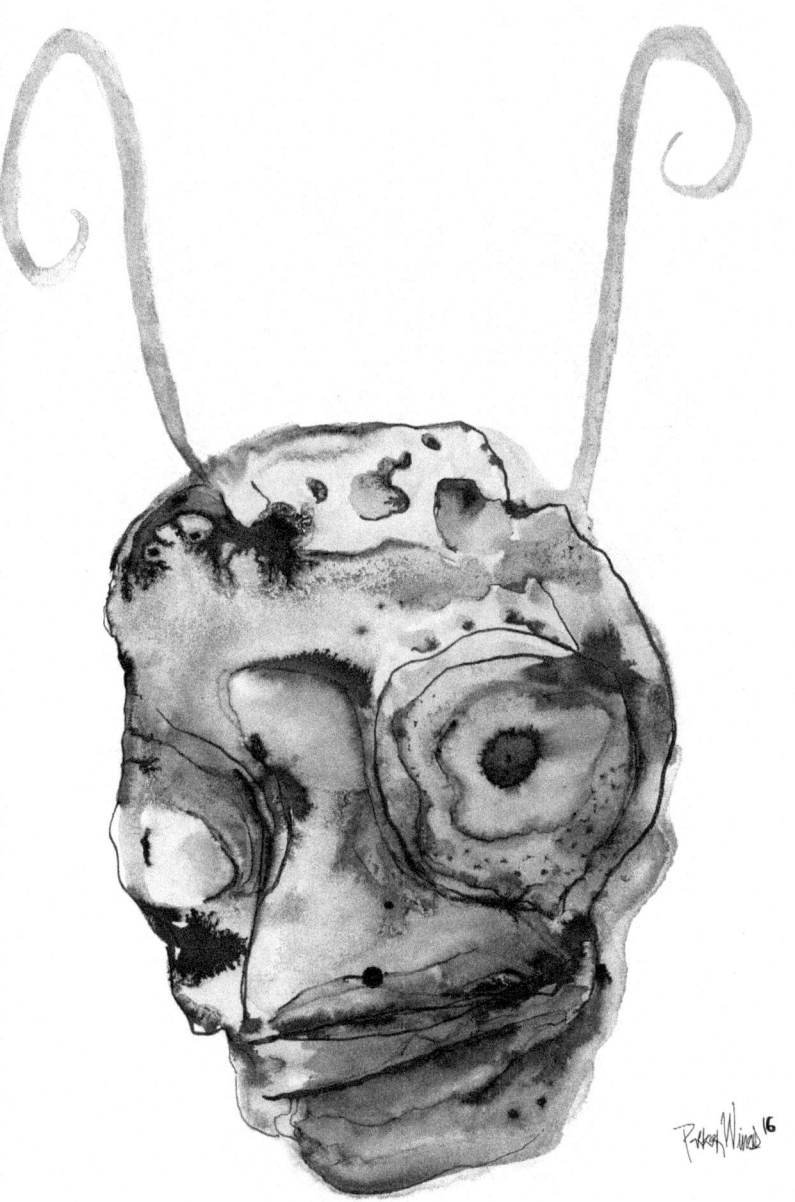

Insectoid

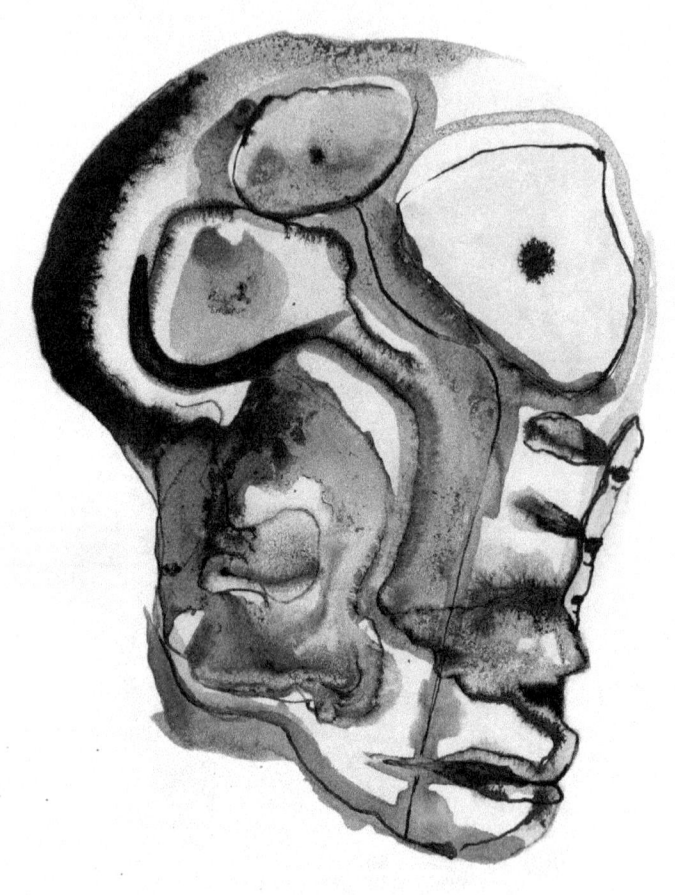

4 AM

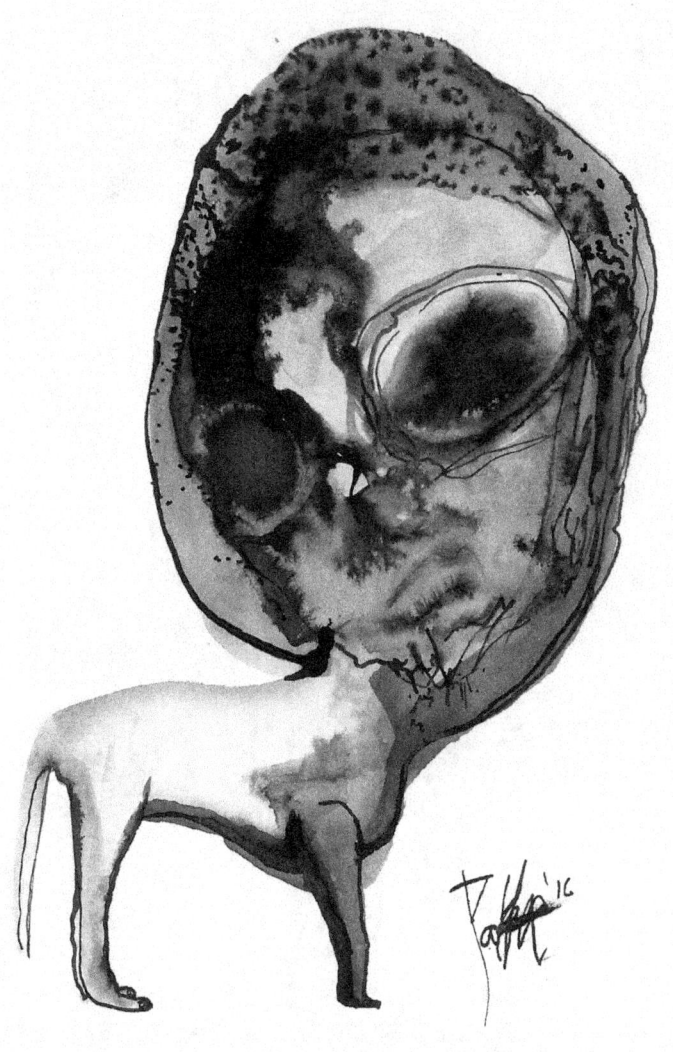

Beast

The one who makes the Mountains

Your Boss

Monster in the Morning

Roots

Feeding Time

The Grinder

The Toaster

Home Again

Meditation is Good

MESSAGE NOTES

SUNDAY MORNING SERVICE

~~Robert Bishop~~ *:: Senior Pastor*

APRIL 10, 2016

PARKER WINANS IS AN AMERICAN ARTIST. HE WAS RAISED IN MINDEN, NEVADA AND LOS ANGELES. HE WANTED TO WRITE THIS PART IN THE FIRST PERSON BECAUSE HE WAS TOLD THAT IT WOULD LOOK ~~UP~~ UNPROFFESSIONAL. HE CURRENTLY LIVES IN LOS ANGELES.

TO LEARN MORE, FOLLOW ON SOCIAL, SEND HAIKUS, BUY ART, ETC. GO TO WWW.PARKERWINANS.COM

© COPYRIGHT 2017 PARKER WINANS

www.ingramcontent.com/pod-product-compliance
Lightning Source LLC
Chambersburg PA
CBHW061442180526
45170CB00004B/1523